# HOW DOES ECHOLOCATION WORK?

Science Book 4th Grade

Children's Science & Nature Books

BABY PROFESSOR

EDUCATION KIDS

Speedy Publishing LLC

40 E. Main St. #1156

Newark, DE 19711

www.speedypublishing.com

Copyright 2017

Using echoes for detection of objects is known as echolocation and can be observed with bats and other creatures. It is also referred to as biosonar. In this book, you will be learning about how it works as well as how it is used by natural creatures as well as by humans.

Echolocating animals send out calls to their environment and then listen for the echoes of calls that return from any object that is near them. These echoes are then used for locating and identifying the objects. It is also used for hunting (foraging) as well as navigation in different environments.

TWO DOLPHINS FROLIC IN THE BLUE CLEAR WATER

Animals that utilize echolocating include a few birds and some mammals, but most notable are the toothed whales and dolphins (odontocetes) and microchiropteran bats. There are also other groups that utilize echolocating in simpler forms, including shrews.

# WHAT IS ECHOLOCATION?

Using echoes and sound waves to determine where an object is located is known as echolocation. Bats are known to use echolocation for finding food and navigating in the dark. Bats send out the sound waves using either their nose or mouth.

BATS

BAT EATING FRUIT

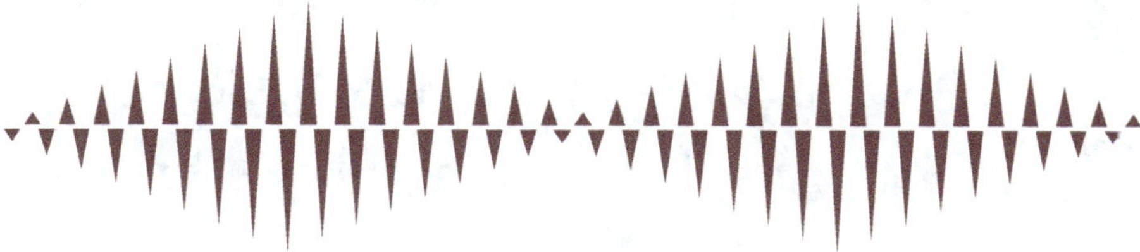

Once the sound waves reach the object, they produce the echoes and the echo then bounces off of the object and returns the signal to the ears of the bat. Bats are then able to figure out from the echo where the object is located, the shape of the object, and the size of the object.

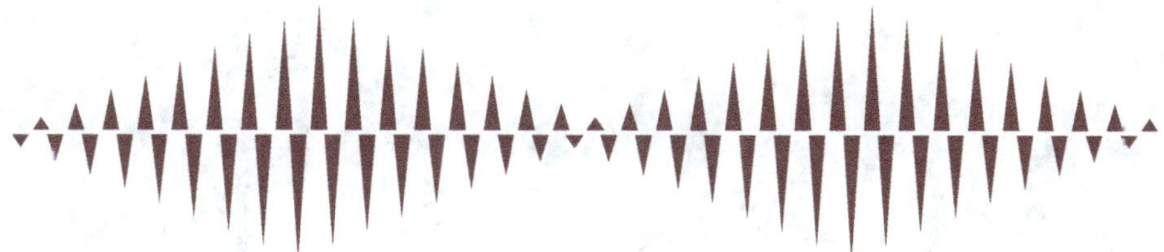

Using the sounds made by the animal itself, echolocating is similar to active sonar. The range is found by the measurement of the delay time occurring between the sound of the animal and the return echoes received from the environment.

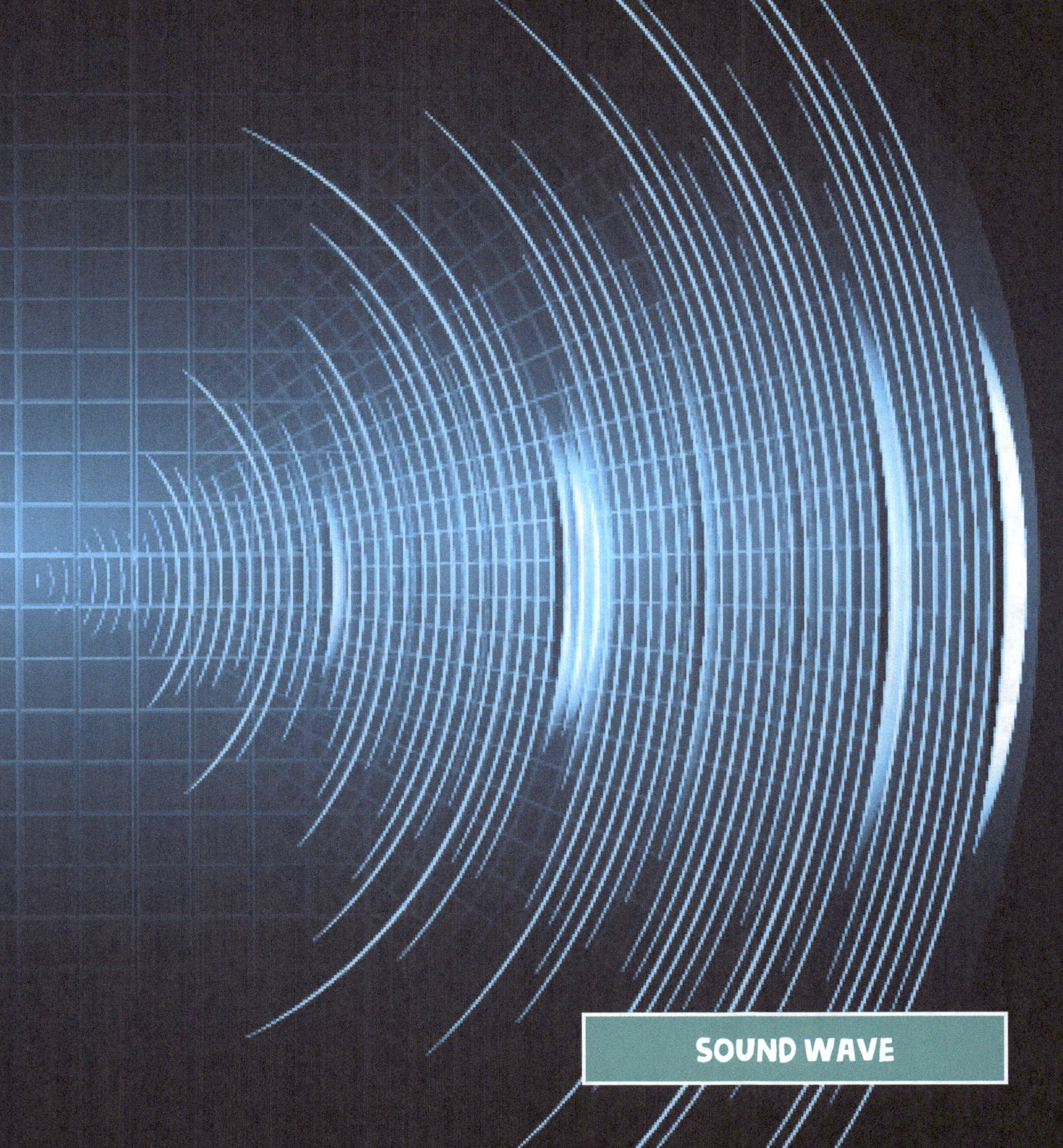
SOUND WAVE

BAT EARS

As well as the sound intensity received by each ear and the time delay between the arrival to the two ears provides the information from where the reflected sound waves arrive.

Unlike some of the sonars made by humans which rely on several narrow beams and receivers to find a target such as a multibeam sonar, echolocation by animals consists of a single transmitter and two receivers, which would be the ears. Echolocating animals have two ears that are slightly positioned apart from each other.

RADAR SEARCHING FOR SOUND

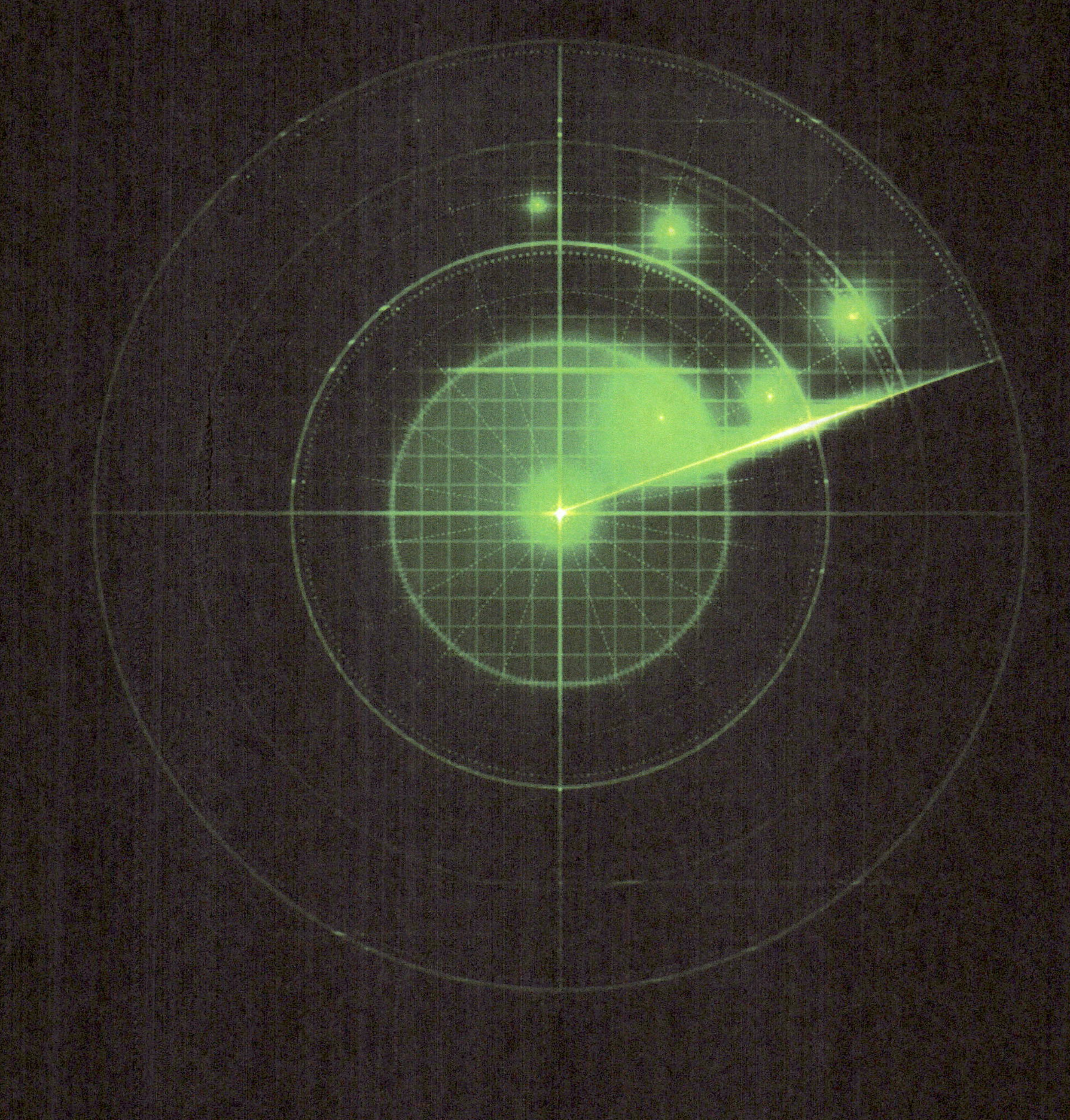

The echoes that return to the two ears then arrive at different times and different levels of loudness, dependent on the object's position that is transmitting the echoes. The animals use the loudness and time differences to perceive the direction and distance. The bat is able to not only see where it is going, but is able to conceive how large the other animal is, what type of animal it is, as well as some of its other features.

SONAR WAVE

# BATS

With the use of echolocation, bats are able to detect objects in complete darkness that are as thin as a strand of human hair. It allows bats to locate insects as small as mosquitoes, which several bats like to eat. Even though bats are not blind, they often use echolocation for finding their way quickly, even in total darkness.

BAT IN A CAVE

YOUNG WOMAN ASSISTING BLIND MAN

# WHAT OTHER ANIMALS USE ECHOLOCATION?

Whales, dolphins, shrews, and some species of birds use echolocation for finding food and for navigation. Blind people have also learned how to use it for navigating throughout their surroundings.

Humans are not able to hear the ultrasonic sounds which the echolocating bats make. However, some insects can hear these sounds, including crickets, beetles, and moths. When a moth hears a bat that is echolocating, some might turn and fly away, while others might start moving in a looping, spiral, or zigzag pattern to throw the echo off and avoid being found by the bat. Some beetles and crickets might make a clicking sound that startles the bat and scares it off to avoid being devoured by the bat.

MOTHS FLYING AROUND A LIGHT BULB

NAVIGATION AND MARINE RADAR ON CAPTAIN'S BRIDGE

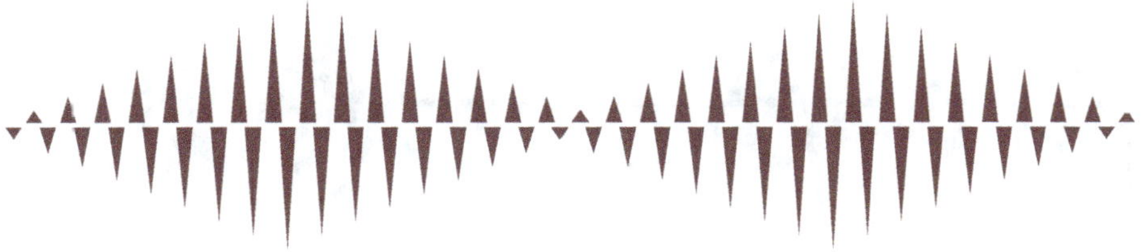

The idea for radar and sonar navigation systems utilized by the military was developed by scientists by studying the echolocation of bats. Like the bats, sonar utilizes sound waves for navigating and locating objects such as ships and submarines. However, sonar is used underwater and bats echolocate throughout the open air.

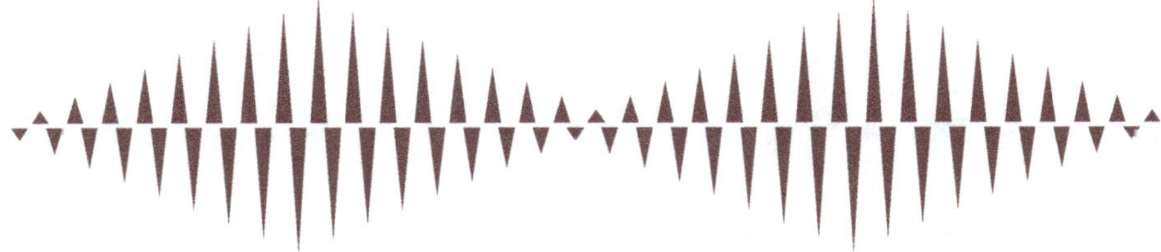

Radar utilizes electromagnetic waves for finding the locations of objects such as ships and planes. Similar to the way a bat uses echolocation, radar is used throughout the open air.

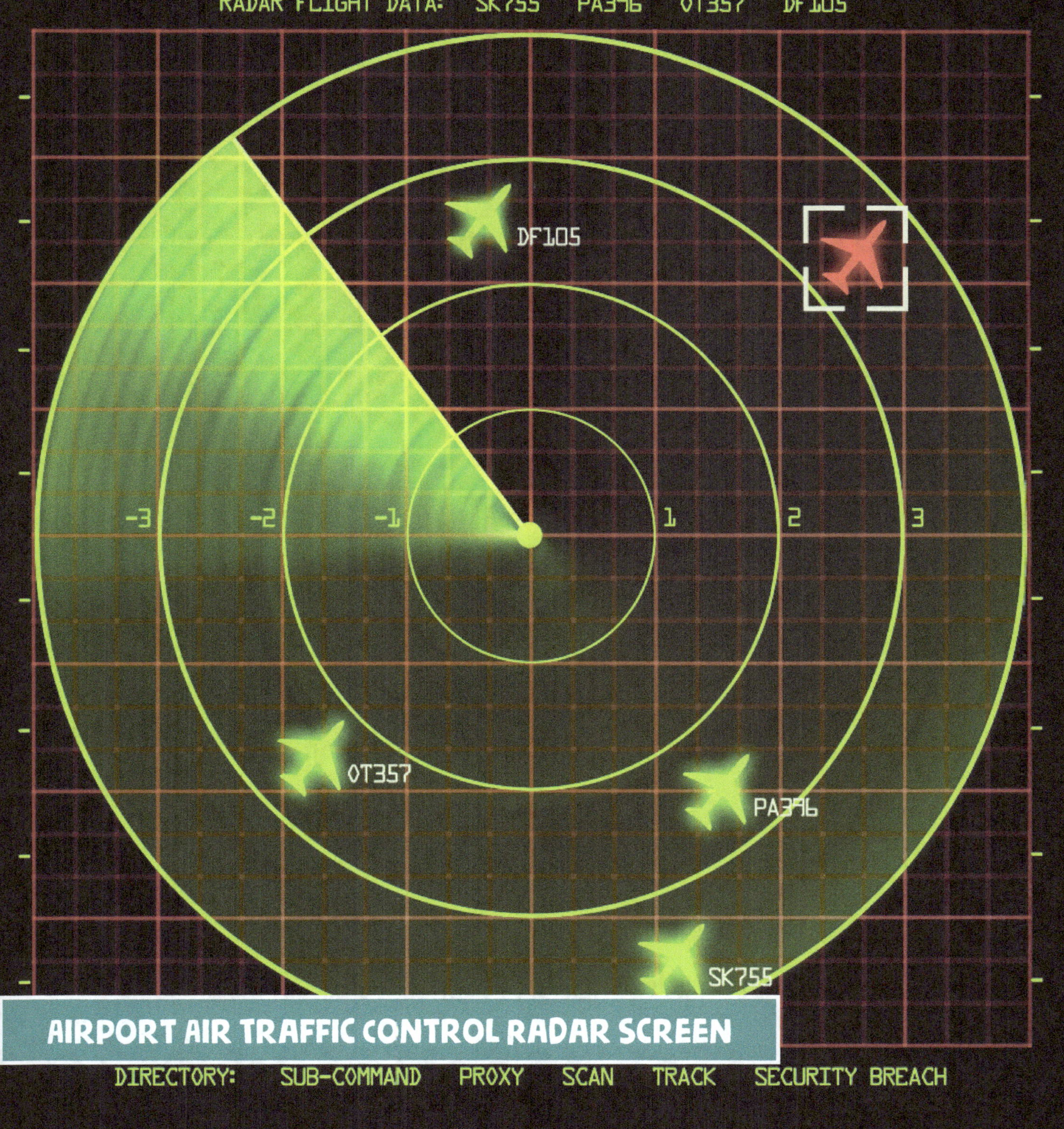

RADAR FLIGHT DATA:    SK755    PA396    OT357    DF105
DF105
-3    -2    -1    1    2    3
OT357
PA396
SK755
AIRPORT AIR TRAFFIC CONTROL RADAR SCREEN
DIRECTORY:    SUB-COMMAND    PROXY    SCAN    TRACK    SECURITY BREACH

# TOOTHED WHALES

Biosonar (echolocation) is a valuable resource to toothed whales, as well as porpoises, sperm whales, dolphins, river dolphins, and killer whales since they live underwater. This environment provides favorable conditions for acoustic characteristics and where their range of vision is extremely limited.

KILLER WHALE PLAYING IN A POOL

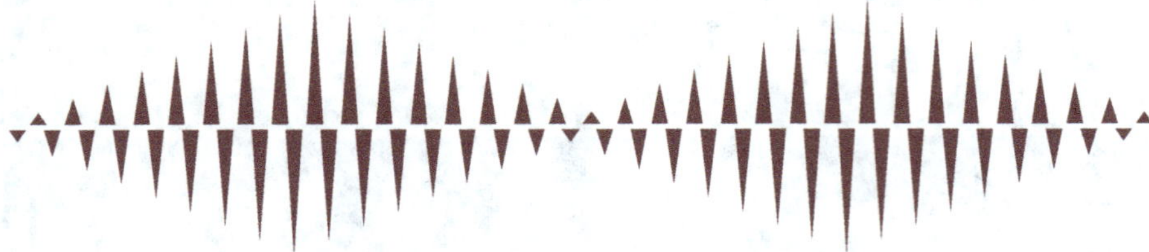

The toothed whale emits a beam of high-frequency clicks towards the same direction their head is facing. Sounds are then generating by passing of air through the phonic lips by the boney nares. The sounds are then reflected by the cranium's concave bone and an air sac situated at its base. The beam is modulated by the "melon" which is a fatty, large organ.

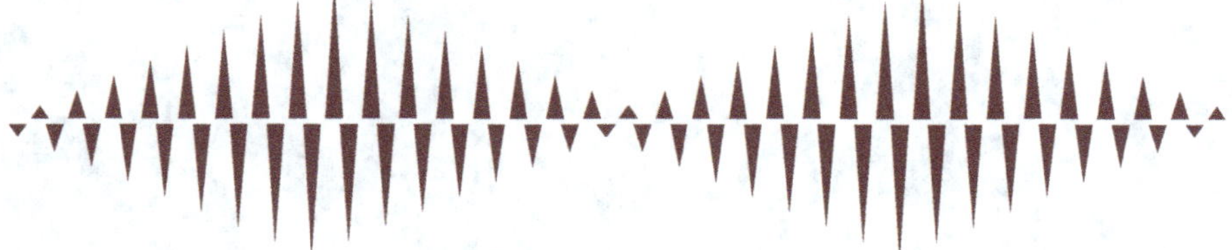

SPERM WHALE

This acts similar to an acoustic lens since it's composed of lipids having differing densities. While a sperm whale might produce individual clicks, most toothed whales will use a series of clicks, otherwise known as a click train, for echolocation. The whistles of the toothed whale don't appear to be used for echolocation.

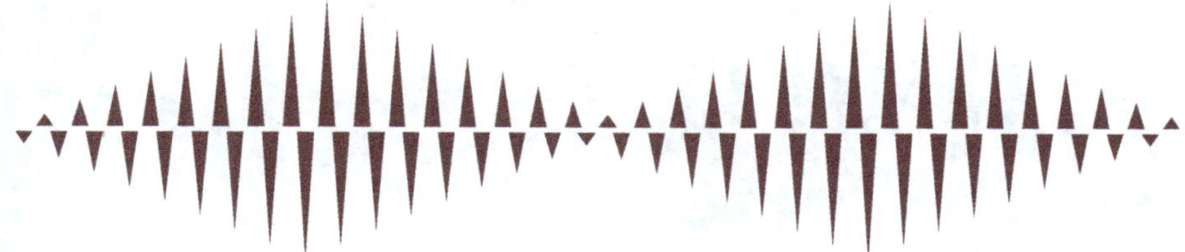

The different click rates produced in a click train create familiar squeals, growls, and barks of the bottlenose dolphin. A burst pulse is a click train consisting of a repetition rate of more than 600 per second, but produces a response for higher rates of repetition.

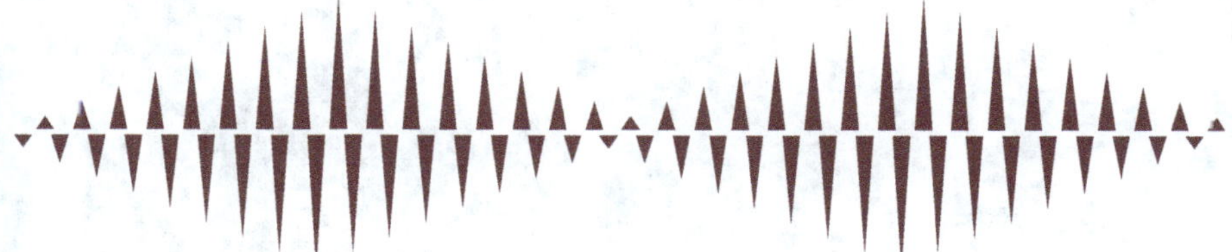

Using complex, fatty structures surrounding the lower jaw as its main reception path, echoes are received to the middle ear by a continuous body of fat. A lateral sound might be received via fatty lobes around the ear having a density similar to water. There are some researchers that believe when the dolphin approaches an object of interest, it will protect itself from the louder echo by quietening the sound that was emitted. This is known to occur with bats, but the hearing sensitivity also may be reduced as it gets closer to the target.

UNDERGROUND RIVER OF PUERTO PRINCESA, PALAWAN, PHILIPPINES

OILBIRDS AND SWIFTLETS

The Palawan swiftlet is able to fly in total darkness inside the Puerto Princesa river cave that is subterranean.

Oilbirds as well as some swiftlet species are known to use a fairly crude echolocation form that compares to that of dolphins and bats. These birds, which are also nocturnal, emit calls as they fly and use these calls to navigate through the caves and trees where they live.

# SHREWS, TENRECS AND RATS

Other terrestrial mammals that are known to echolocate include the Sorex and Blarina, which are two of the genera of the shrews, as well as the tenrecs of Madagascar. The shrew sounds different than bats and are broadband, frequency modulated, multi-harmonic, and low amplitude.

MADAGASCAR TENREC

A HUNTING COMMON SHREW

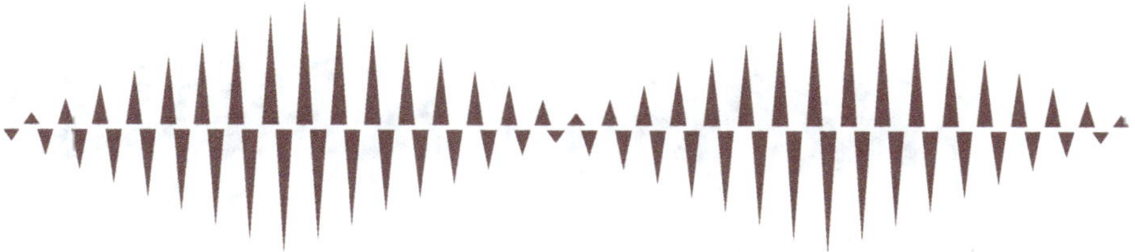

They do not contain any "echolocation clicks" with reverberations and seems only to be used only for simple, close range spatial orientation. Shrews only use echolocation for investigating their habitat and do not use it to find food.

There is proof that laboratory rats that are blinded are able to use echolocation in navigating mazes.

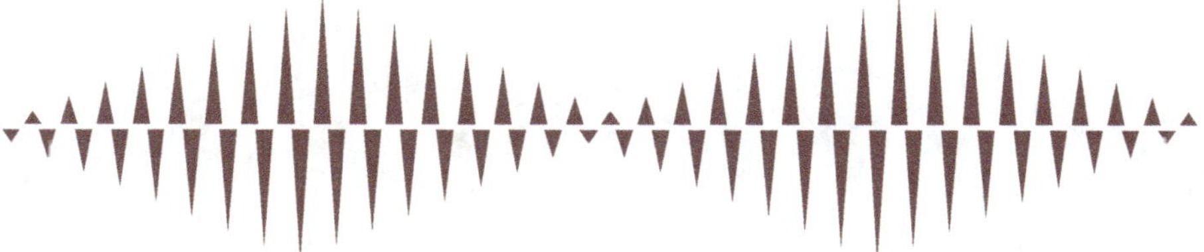

# HUMAN ECHOLOCATION

The ability of a human in detecting objects by sensing echoes received from the object is human echolocation. This is done by actively creating a sound such as snapping the fingers, making a clicking noise using their mouth, lightly stomping the foot, or tapping their cane.

People have been trained to interpret these sound waves that are reflected by an object that is close by the use of echolocation, and are able to accurately identify its size and location.

Some blind people use this ability for navigating their environment with the use of auditory cues rather than visual cues. This is similar to the principle in active sonar and animal echolocation, used by bats, toothed whales, and bats for finding their prey.

Hearing and vision are related closely since they have the ability to process reflected energy waves. Vision processes the light waves as they move from the source, bounce off of the surfaces throughout the environment, and then enters the eyes.

The auditory system, similarly, processes the sound waves as they move from their source, bounce of the surfaces, and then enter the ears.

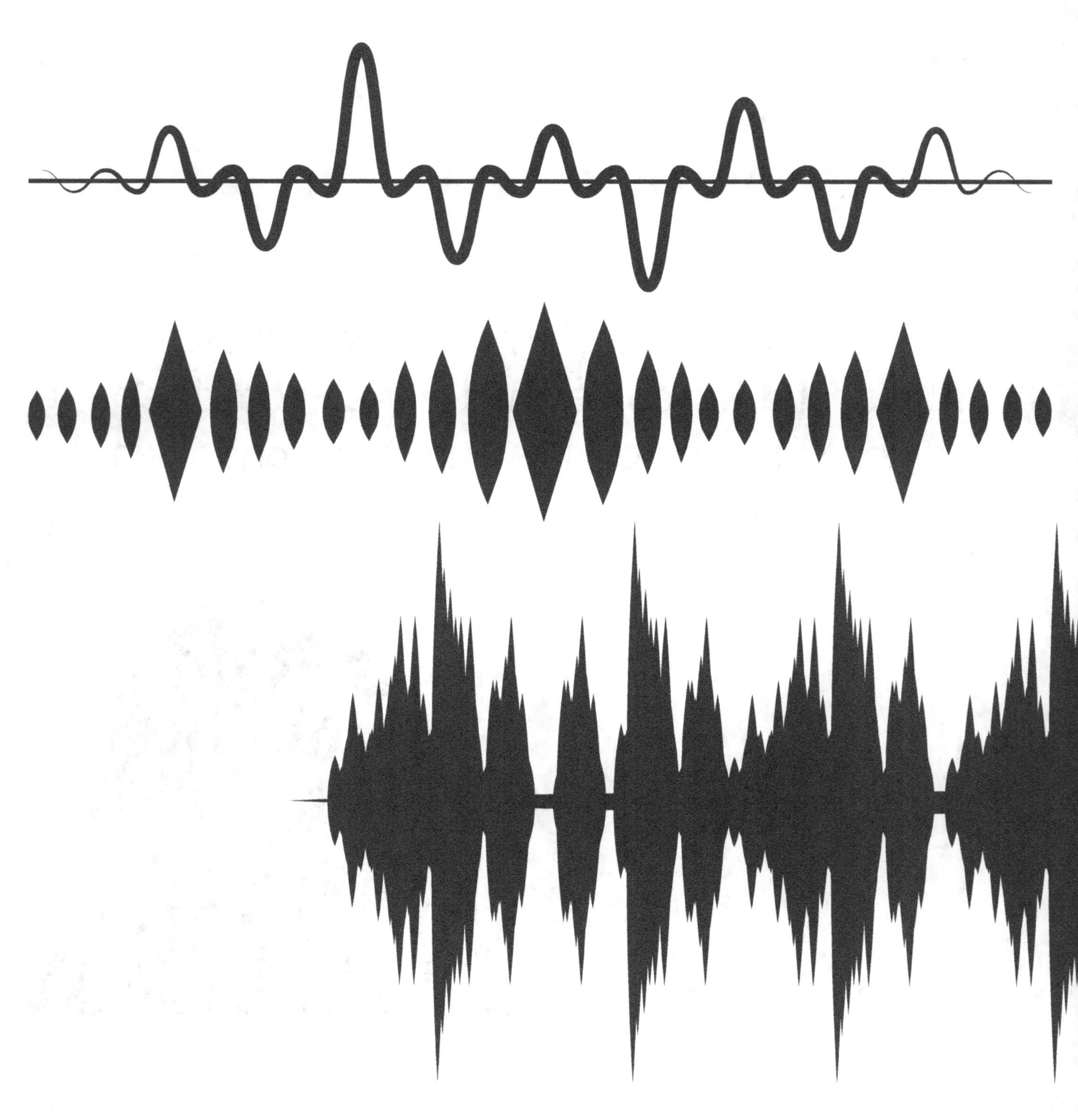

Both of these systems can obtain a huge amount of information regarding the environment by interpreting the patterns of energy that they have received. In the instance of sound, the reflected energy waves are known as "echoes".

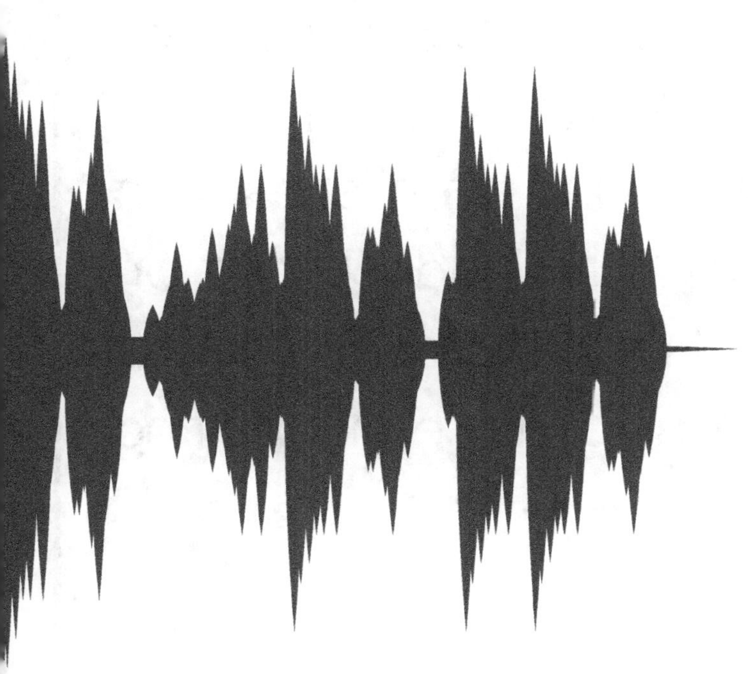

# ECHOLOCATION JAMMING

Animal echolocation systems, similar to human radar systems, can be susceptible to interference which is referred to as echolocation jamming. This occurs when a non-target sound interferes with the target echoes. This can be inadvertent or purposeful, and can result from the echolocation system on its own, or various other echolocating animals, prey, or humans.

BOY COVERING HIS EYES

The animals' use of echolocation has evolved to minimize the jamming, but the avoidance is not successful all of the time.

Echolocation is utilized in many ways by several different species of animals in order to survive. Try it out for yourself - close your eyes and listen for a sound and then determine where it is coming from. If you were able to figure out where the sound was coming from, you used echolocation.

For additional information about echolocation, you can visit your local library, research the internet, and ask questions of you teachers, family, and friends.

Visit

BABY PROFESSOR
EDUCATION KIDS

# www.BabyProfessorBooks.com

to download Free Baby Professor eBooks
and view our catalog of new and exciting
Children's Books